the
haikus

bob wells

For Linnie and Leander Deniz

PROLOGUE

Last December, I was looking for a new creative challenge for the upcoming year. In the past several years, I've typically tried my hand at learning a new language, or completing some study program.

I chanced upon an article posted on CNN by Tess Taylor. In it, Taylor wrote about how her practice of writing a haiku daily unlocked greater creativity and energy within her.

I immediately felt a surge of energy and creativity, and I was excited to start my own daily practice of writing a haiku and eventually publish them. What follows is a collection of those haikus for you to enjoy.

Like life, I hope that these haikus will also make you think about what is today, as well as be hopeful about tomorrow. More importantly, I hope that they will inspire each of you to chase your dreams.

13 Nissan, 5783   Bob Wells
April 4, 2023

kisses from her lips
were like drugs i couldn't quit
"once more" i begged her

on the wings of hope
dreams soar reaching for heaven
whilst lifting us up

this new year brings hope
to make the world better off
for all those we love

under the rubble
a voice of defiance screams
"i will survive this"

today came early
its quietness beckoning
get started my son

hope springs eternal
urging us to move forward
and carpe diem

family and friends
are ties that bind provide love
support us each day

the daily mundane
is anything but if we
simply look closer

january 6th
need not bring more of the same
old rancor and hate

shabbos day of rest
a chance to recharge refresh
with loved ones and friends

the grand ole party
tattered and in disarray
need a new leader

the quiet wakes me
before the city can roar
whispering let's go

pictures can move us
they're more than a thousand words
they are hopes goals dreams

unexamined lives
bring regret sadness and more
the cure is purpose

nuance a lost art
replaced by virtue signals
obfuscating truth

*anger has a place
for broken men and women
clinging to the past*

the road less traveled
is often a lonely one
which requires courage

"too risky" she said
as she walked out on our love
trembling as she left

what is it to dream
to dare for a brave new world
or perchance just sleep

as she breathed her last,
he softly whispered to her
"goodbye my angel"

Freeman Henderson [1]
the prince with the golden voice
calls games for G-d now

the 'Merican dream
an illusory promise
saved for just a few

the eve of the storm
marked by a feeling of calm
masks what is to come

providence charming
and a gem of the east coast
land full of mensches

on the wings of hope
sunday morning brings us all
a chance to start fresh

where will you live now
in a misremembered past
unknown tomorrows

brief moments in time
are precious gifts for us all
to share with loved ones

beauty surrounds us
we need only choose to see
and bask in its glow

exploring the world
means embracing fear and change
to discover self

time does not stand still
like it we must march ahead
and not look backwards

don't give up too soon
fight for what matters to you
tomorrow yet comes

the path to regret
it begins with unchased dreams
and ends bitterly

imagination
a gift to us as children
to nurture each day

Очень красивый,
Как закат на пляже
В конце для

ignorance enchants
siren song of nescience
music to some ears

gib mir deine hand
unsere Zukunft wartet
wir müssen gehen

i can sense them near
icy winds ready to pounce
and claim "winter's here"

the flames engulf me
their crackle warning taunting
calling "be afraid"

questioning yourself
blessing curse path to the truth
you alone decide

*wisdom is the key
to growth perhaps happiness
it is true power*

la dulce vida
salud riquezas amor
o un gran libro

if these walls could talk
would they speak of death or hope
inspire or warn us

la dulce vida
salud riquezas amor
o un gran libro

if these walls could talk
would they speak of death or hope
inspire or warn us

hider or seeker
when bold action is required
which role will you play

like Maya, i rise
to face the day's challenges
poised in my black skin

antakya cries out
begging the world to notice
what they truly face

what is it all for
to feel like you're more secure
to impress someone

zero dark thirty
the best time to start the day
and make time for you

time will heal all wounds
even our life's greatest scars
just the scabs remain

alles im einklang
die beste Art zu leben
oder nur ein wunsch

why are dreams deferred
did we not work hard enough
or were they stolen

last night i missed you
not for the last time either
my precious angel

each time something new
friends memories sights sounds smells
istanbul you rule

a man's tenderness
as sign of weakness or strength
depends on your view

i want to feel more
peace love joy and happiness
and less strife and pain

a walk in the woods
gives us a chance to recharge
and enjoy nature

the day that she left
will live on in infamy
oh what might have been

the need for others
is something that we all share
in this we are one

how can you measure
the amount of hope you have
in smiles or in tears

the empire's last gasp
a war for truth and freedom
is now at our feet

kalamazoo's zoo
is a place full of wonder
according to Jim

que lo viene
es bonito o feo
quién lo sabe

the magic of hope
lies in its ability
to inspire us all

our children are our ___
blessing curse frustration hope
what does your lens say

what defines a man
is not what's between his legs
but between his ears

how can I find love
finding ways to share my life
or something deeper

watching her sleep now
is the greatest of blessings
one day she'll know why

the darkness calls me
enticing me to let go
and be swallowed whole

my home is no more
it probably never was
and was just a dream

why does it hurt so
do I deserve this somehow
or it's how life works

i refuse to quit
despite my slim chance with her
why stop fighting now

the good doctor cried
as he walked in to tell us
he couldn't save her

he was terrified
the woods always felt so dark
and full of evil

"don't ever give up"
that was the message from Jim
as he fought like hell

despair quickly mounts
as the body count rises
L-rd! what have you done

she sat there and smiled
as the men walked by and stared
"damn i'm fine" she mused

what made him give up
was it black skin or thin skin
or fear of fighting

"hope springs eternal"
that's what she used to tell me
Sliva i miss you

a walk to forget
to erase the pain and scars
of her leaving us

he nervously smiled
as his students approached him
they could sense his fear

irrational thoughts
bounced all around in his head
fitting for pi day

"let her go" he thought
he would no longer be hurt
as she chose others

fear of failure is
strong in adults but not kids
unless we teach them

"win the day" he says
keep the focus on the now
and don't look ahead

we all know someone
who is spiteful and bitter
what a waste of life

"she never loved you"
"and I know this hurts" he thought
"try to forget her"

why should you fight on
if you know what you are worth
how could you give up

"it could be much worse"
he told himself fighting tears
"they could all be dead"

oh liebe Karen
und was hast du jetzt gemacht
der chef ist nicht da

take time for yourself
to stop and 'smell the roses'
or whatever else

"time heals all" they say
but i don't believe that's true
since I still feel pain

take time for yourself
to stop and 'smell the roses'
or whatever else

"time heals all" they say
but i don't believe that's true
since I still feel pain

why do we fear truth
are we afraid of what's next
or of the mirror

i'm afraid of love
you made me that way i think
what do i do now

you must not forget
he always believed in you
his dreams your greatness [2]

unreturned letters
were they read or just received
what does it matter

the monster is near
only it's not a monster
and instead just fear

without you life sucks
you were my reason to live
to love and to fight

breadcrumbs lead to you
tempting nay tantalizing
despite their poison

the grey clouds appear
obscuring the light from me
when will the sun come

gasping for my breath
i turn to you to save me
yet you walk away

the pain of loss burns
searing scars onto my heart
thank g-d you are near

when is tomorrow
you say it's not much longer
you've said that before

"i care" her first lie
followed by an avalanche
of deceitfulness

my dream vacation
sandy beach epic ruins
no it's time with you

character matters
until it no longer does
we all lose that day

possibilities
breathed to life by each new day
urge me to act soon

Leander Deniz
you're the wind beneath my wings
ma raison d'être

she gently whispered
too soft to be overhead
"i've always loved you"

as the thunder rolled
i mused "what would Garth do now"
would he nap or sing

your father dreamed too
and then you came from heaven
a gift from the g-ds

*ich vermisse dich
und ich kann nicht warten mehr
ich muss dich sehen*

ACKNOWLEDGEMENTS

*African cultures maintain that "It takes a village..."
to do anything significant. This was a significant
project for me on multiple levels, so I want to take
the time to thank my tribe, all of my villages, and
their citizens, who have helped me to get to this
place. Unfortunately, some of them are no longer
with us in this world, but they and their families
have my eternal gratitude and respect.*

*First of all, I want to thank MY tribe: Linnie, Bob,
Fay, Nick, Leander Deniz, Grandmother Saunders,
Mama Mary, Big Daddy, Pearl, James, Zeke,
Dean, Loomis, Buck, Sylvester, Louise, Bernie,
Tatia, Yolanda, Sylvia, Mark,
You each have supported me, challenged me, and
motivated me to work hard, dream big, and
always strive to be the best version of myself
possible. I am eternally humbled and grateful for
your support.*

*I also want to thank my Murfreesboro and Duke
villages: Roger Featherston, David Bennett, Tom
Jones, Ben Williamson, Bruno Sanchez, Shane
Branch, Fred Goldsmith, Ken Matous, Josh
Danziger, Rabbi Lew, Dawud Rasheed, Desi
Thomas, Ethan Fricklas, Doctor Rabbi Kalman
Bland, and last, but definitely not least Dean
Martina J. Bryant.
On and off the gridiron, you have provided me
with so many valuable lessons that I still carry*

with me today. Words can only begin to express my gratitude.

To my villages in Massachusetts, New York, and across the globe: the amazing team over at Taryag Publishing, Miss Julie, Othamian "Thamey" Peterson, Karolinka Pawlak, Lukas Horn, Michael ʼ Marcus, Bert Margolis, Mayor Dan, Julia Longthorne, Annie, Erin, Mike Bayani, Matt "All About the K.C." Plotkin, Dr. Lubetkin, Justin Foley, Michael Granger, Rabbi Zali, Martina Tormoche, Eli Damatov, Rod McClave, Rabbi Josef Davis, Sari Steinberg, Milos Litman, Rabbi Yitschak Asiel, William Ehrman, Candan and the rest of the Saydam crew, and Rachel Waldman.
Thank you each for sharing with me your enduring wisdom and individually unique views of the world.

I am incredibly fortunate to have so many people in so many cities and countries around the world to be grateful for. Therefore, I have no doubt forgotten to thank someone, and I apologize deeply for that oversight.

Last, but certainly not least, I want to thank you, the reader. I am incredibly grateful that you have chosen to purchase this book, but I'm even more grateful for the time that you took from your busy schedule and life to read it. I hope you enjoyed reading it as much as I enjoyed writing it.

NOTES

[1] Freeman Henderson was the longtime radio announcer for the Murfreesboro Rattlers sports teams in Murfreesboro, Arkansas. I fondly remember his incredible kindness and graciousness, as well as him checking in with me when I was at Duke. Those who remember Freeman Henderson will also have stories of his kindness and how he touched their lives in some meaningful way.

[2] This haiku was inspired by my late friend and high school teammate, Bruno Sanchez. Sadly, he passed away after a traffic accident in March 2023. As a 9th grader, I remember being awed by his athletic potential. More recently, I was awed by his belief in everyone else's potential, and his desire for them to achieve their potential.